DREAMS AND VISIONS

God's Picture Language for the Heart

JENNIFER TRUESDALE

ISBN 979-8-88616-164-9 (paperback)
ISBN 979-8-88616-165-6 (digital)

Christian Faith Publishing
832 Park Avenue
Meadville, PA 16335
www.christianfaithpublishing.com

Printed in the United States of America

To my children, Angela and Marcus.

The best daughter and son a mother could ever hope for, I feel truly blessed.

Contents

Acknowledgment

With special thanks to my husband for his support and patience.

I would also like to acknowledge Don Cason, pastor of Hope Chapel, a Foursquare church in Owasso, Oklahoma, for his help in the final editing.

Introduction

This is a collection of dreams and visions I received from God the Father through his Holy Spirit, after I received Jesus into my heart as my personal Lord and Savior. Some of these dreams and visions I have shared with my friends, and some I have pondered in my heart over the years. Recently I have felt compelled to write a few of the dreams and visions down onto paper and comment on each one. These are not all the dreams and visions I have received over the years but are those I feel might have a special significance to others. It is my prayer that these dreams and visions may bring freedom, hope, and comfort to all who read them and salvation to those who do not know Jesus as their Lord and Savior.

Many people who read this book may think that it contains dreams and visions that have no meaning. They may even say to themselves, "God doesn't speak that way today." They may even try to explain them by saying, "When the Bible was finished, God didn't need to speak to us in dreams and visions anymore. We now have his Holy Word, the Bible, and that's how he speaks to us." I would like to say this, "Yes, God does speak to us through his Word, the Bible, but there are times when we may not fully comprehend his word. He then speaks his word in a language of pictures." This picture language is similar to the language he used to teach the crowds who gathered to listen to him; he spoke to them in parables, such as in Mathew 13:3 (NIV). God may choose to speak to us in a variety of different ways. One of the ways he may speak to us is in a dream or vision. Even though dreams and visions are not parables, some have parabolic roots because they convey symbolic pictures that help us to understand spiritual truths. I would like to challenge anyone who thinks that God does not speak to us through dreams and visions to read their bibles. Here are a few verses that you may wish to read:

"And afterward, I will pour out my Spirit on all people. Your sons and daughters will prophesy, your old men will dream dreams, your young men will see visions. Even on my servants, both men and women, I will pour out my Spirit in those days" (Joel 2:28–29 NIV).

"One day at about three in the afternoon he had a vision. He distinctly saw an angel of God, who came to him and said, 'Cornelius!' Cornelius stared at him in fear. 'What is it, Lord?' he asked" (Acts 10:3–4 NIV).

"Then the Lord came down in a pillar of cloud; he stood at the entrance to the Tent and summoned Aaron and Miriam. When both of them stepped forward, he said, 'Listen to my words. When a prophet of the Lord is among you, I reveal myself to him in visions, I speak to him in dreams. But this is not true of my servant Moses; he is faithful in all my house. With him I speak face to face, clearly and not in riddles. He sees the form of the Lord'" (Numbers 12:5–8 NIV).

"One night the Lord spoke to Paul in a vision. 'Do not be afraid. Keep on speaking, do not be silent. For I am with you, and no one is going to attack and harm you because I have many people in this city'" (Acts 18:9–10 NIV).

This is my hope and prayer as you read these dreams and visions. I pray God's Holy Spirit will anoint your hearts and minds to understand one of the ways God may choose to speak. It is my desire for anyone, who reads these dreams and visions, to realize that God does speak to us in various ways. He speaks through his Holy Spirit to our hearts and minds and through his Word, the Bible. He also speaks to our hearts and minds by his Holy Spirit through dreams and visions. God's Holy Spirit is the person who teaches us all things, in whatever way he chooses.

A Dream of Salvation

I had a dream that my husband and I were on a journey. The road we were traveling on was very wide and smooth. It appeared to be paved, yet it also seemed to be a dirt road. This road was in the middle of nowhere. Nothing else seemed to be in sight except this long wide road. Traveling along this desolate road, we soon approached a gate located across the entire width of the road. This gate was tall and wide, and on the inside, there were workers positioned on either side of the gate. There appeared to be a watchtower off to the left side just inside the entrance. The tower was occupied by workers with weapons—rifles of some kind. The place beyond the gate looked somewhat like a prison camp with an eight-foot-high chain-linked fence surrounding it. The fence was topped with strands of barbed wire. The gate would open as people neared the entrance to this place allowing them to enter the compound. Upon entering, workers would shut and lock the gate so that it was not possible to leave once you had set foot inside the camp. Warily, my husband and I entered. I became very distressed by the reality that once we came in, we would not be allowed to leave. This was extremely frightening. I felt a sense of hopelessness and fear. At this precise moment, I realized that this place *was* a prison camp. While we stood just inside the gate, I became aware of three buildings to my right. Occasionally, someone would go through the gateway of the center building but would not return to the camp. Observing this, I became curious and told my husband to come with me to find out what was going on in these buildings. I was scared but at the same time, I felt a feeling of hope.

We started walking toward the buildings when I noticed, instead of three separate buildings, the buildings blended and became as one with a gateway in the center. We stood for a moment and watched as two people went through the gateway. Curiously we followed them. Once we were inside, I observed that it resembled an ancient gateway to a city. The building was made of stone and the gateway was arched and there was no door. We walked through the gateway of the buildings when suddenly we became aware of the fact that we were no longer in the prison camp. We were free! I said to myself, "That was so simple. Why doesn't anyone else realize they don't have to stay in that prison any longer? All they have to do is go through the gateway of the building to be free. I guess most people just want to make things more complicated than what they really are."

Comment

Many of us find ourselves imprisoned by our way of life. We think that we are on the right road in life, but to our dismay, find ourselves in bondage. "There is a way that seems right to a man, but in the end, it leads to death" (Proverbs 14:12 NIV). Jesus said in Matthew:

"Enter through the narrow gate. For wide is the gate and broad is the road that leads to destruction, and many enter through it. But small is the gate and narrow the road that leads to life, and only a few find it" (Matthew 7:12–14 NIV).

This pathway of our life is typically smooth, but leaves us with the stain of sin just like a dirt road will leave us covered in dust and grime. It is, for the most part, a barren and lonely road for most of us. We keep going because we do not know what else to do. To turn back seems just as hopeless and desolate as continuing to travel forward. "Father, forgive them, for they do not know what they are doing" (Luke 23:34 NIV). This seems like the only course we can take and we stay on it, hoping this road will lead us somewhere. To our dismay, the path we choose leads us to our imprisonment. We become entangled by ourselves, the affairs, and things of this world. When we become imprisoned, we feel stuck there with no possibility of escape. There is hope though for those of us who find ourselves in bondage, no matter what the bondage may be for our particular life. There is continually a gateway open for us through which we may obtain freedom. "For the wages of sin is death, but the gift of God is eternal life in Christ Jesus our Lord" (Romans 6:23 NIV), and "…for everyone who calls on the name of the Lord will be saved" (Romans 10:13 NIV). This gateway is usually right in front of our eyes, but many of us cannot see it because it is too simple. We want to work our way to freedom in a more complicated way. Jesus said in Matthew, "I tell you the truth, unless you change and become like little children, you will never enter the kingdom of heaven" (Matthew 18:3 NIV).

How many of us, having been bound by our way of life, have had someone tell us "Jesus Christ died upon the cross for our sins", but we then reject that message as too simple? The gateway to life is always before us, especially when we feel we have reached the end of the road and have no hope left. When we feel entangled and trapped by our choices in life it is up to us to choose whether we want to open our hearts and receive our salvation. We don't need to reason or question. We just need to accept the gateway of life for what it is, and pass through it, so that we may be free. We cannot let fear rule our hearts. We must open our hearts to the hope that is in Christ Jesus. We need to act when the opportunity to be free is presented to us. "In the time of my favor, I heard you and in the day of salvation, I helped you. I tell you now is the time of God's favor, now is the day of salvation" (2 Corinthians 6:2 NIV). If we do not take advantage of the opportunity to go through the gateway of hope, we will stay in a place of hopelessness. We will forever feel trapped and imprisoned. In John 10:1–10 (NIV), Jesus talks about being the gate of the sheep. It would be best to read the whole chapter, but here I will only give two verses:

"I am the gate; whoever enters through me will be saved. He will come in and go out, and find pasture. The thief comes only to steal, and kill, and destroy, I have come that they may have life and have it to the full" (John 10:9–10 NIV).

In conclusion, I would like to ask those who have heard the message of salvation, but find it too simple to accept to stop and take note of your life. Have you reached the end of your rope? Does your life seem meaningless? Have you tried everything complicated you could think of to make yourself happy but still find that your life is empty and you are imprisoned by it? If so, will you at least now look to the simple answer? What have you got left to lose? Although the demons of hell have shut the gates on you, do not let them deceive you any longer. Yes, you are imprisoned, but you don't have to stay there. The workers of hell may have shut the gates, but Jesus offers a way of escape. When you finally make the decision to accept Jesus, you will experience the freedom and peace your heart so desperately seeks.

"That if you confess with your mouth, Jesus is Lord, and believe in your heart that God raised him from the dead, you will be saved. For it is with your heart that you believe and are justified, and it is with your mouth you confess and are saved" (Romans 10:9–10 NIV).

A Vision of the Preparation of the Gospel of Peace

One day, as I was lying in bed praying, I received a vision. I saw myself sitting on a wall made of stone that stood about two-feet high. Sitting on the wall, my feet were able to touch the ground. I did not have any shoes on and was completely alone; I was crying uncontrollably. Suddenly, a man came and stood next to me. He was not handsome and did not have any features that would cause me to notice him. He seemed like an average person, not extremely beautiful, and yet he wasn't ugly. He was dressed in the type of clothing ancient Hebrews or Israelites might have worn—a bone or camel hair colored robe with a coarse rope belt about his waist and leather sandals.

He looked at me and asked me why I was crying. Looking up at him through teary eyes, I replied, "No one will believe me. They're all so evil and such hypocrites." I began to cry again. He then looked up at me and said, "Go and put your shoes on and start digging a fence post hole." I felt like he was not only saying fence post hole, but also a post hole for a mailbox. Both seemed to be in my mind when he spoke. I was startled when he said this because although he talked in a normal pitched voice, I could feel the authority and power in his words. I knew I had to do what he commanded. The authority and power that my whole being felt when he spoke made me realize that it would be very difficult to resist by not obeying. I knew this man was Jesus.

He then moved about five feet away from me and waited for me to answer. I stood up and went to him arguing the whole time and in a sense, pleading with him about this. I just could not go. He did not answer me. He just stood there patiently waiting. I continued to cry and tell him, "I cannot go because no one believes me. They're all so evil, and they're all hypocrites, liars, etc." He remained totally silent and continued looking at me with an authoritative expression. I realized he would not take no for an answer. After that, he seemed to become filled with compassion because he took me in his arms to comfort me. Holding me closely, he remained very still, not speaking. I continued to sob and cry. I then became defensive and told him I could not do what he commanded. Unexpectedly, it seemed like the power and authority of the words he had spoken to me earlier struck me forcefully in my spirit. Instantly I gained a newfound strength and power seemed to enter my being. I stood back and declared to him, "I'll go. I'll do as you have said." Before I had a chance to leave, he looked at me again and said, "When evil comes upon you, it comes not upon you to fight against you, but comes upon you to fight against me for I am within you. It is trying to defeat me all over again, but fear not for I have overcome the world. I defeated it once and for all when I died upon the cross and rose to power on the third day. I do not have to defeat it again. Fear not."

I immediately found myself standing in the yard on the side of the house. The house was on the same property as the wall. I began digging with a shovel. When I started to dig, a bee came upon me and began buzzing about my head. I became frightened and quit digging. My concentration was on the bee, and I recognized the bee represented evil. I reached my hand up over my head and caught the bee, squishing it between my fingers. I threw it force-fully to the ground thinking it was dead and then picked up my shovel to begin digging again. The bee was still lying at my feet when all of a sudden, life entered the bee, and it soon began flying about my head as if it had never been dead. Several times I would reach up, grab the bee, squish it between my fingers, and throw it to the ground. I thought I had killed it each time, but came to the realization it would not die. The bee then terrified me even more because it flew down the neck of my dress and down along my back. I was afraid that it would sting me. I clearly understood I could not defeat it by myself. If I could only find Jesus, whom I had talked with earlier. I started to search for him when to my surprise, he was immediately right there in front of me about six or seven feet away. The bee was still buzzing about my head as I looked at Jesus. Jesus looked back at me with anger in his expression. I became amazed with the realization that his anger was not directed at me, instead his anger was directed at the bee. His anger was so intense that a beam of light came from his eyes and consumed the bee, leaving nothing left of it but ashes. When the bee came upon me, I could not perceive him near me. My eyes had become so blinded by my thoughts of the bee attacking me; I had completely forgotten it was not my fight. If I had kept my eyes on Jesus and concentrated on the work he commanded me to do, I would not have wasted so much time fighting something I could not defeat on my own.

Comment

I feel that many young Christians experience a time in their lives when no one listens to them. They try, to no avail, to tell people about Jesus. They may feel God is calling them to preach the Gospel even if it is only to their own family and friends. The putting on of shoes in the vision represents a part of the armor of God talked about in Ephesians 6:15 (NIV), "…and with your feet fitted with the readiness that comes from the Gospel of peace." As in the vision, many times in our daily lives, Jesus comes to us not in his resurrection glory, but as an ordinary man. He comes as someone whom we can look upon and call our friend without the feeling of guilt and without becoming afraid. He commands us to preach the Good News, but we do not always want to obey. Past failures or difficulties with people make us hesitant about sharing the Gospel story, so we become unwilling to go out again and share the Gospel with others.

After much arguing and crying within ourselves, we go because we know that we must. In deciding to do the work that Jesus has called us to do, we gain new strength, by the power in his word, through his Holy Spirit. To prepare ourselves we need to dig into the word of God. He does not send us without warning us about the powers of darkness that shall try to come against us as we prepare to do the will of God. A couple of these warnings are:

"I am sending you out like sheep among wolves. Therefore, be as shrewd as snakes and as innocent as doves" (Matthew 10:16 NIV).

"For our struggle is not against flesh and blood, but against the rulers, against the authorities, against the powers of this dark world, and against the spiritual forces of evil in the heavenly realms" (Ephesians 6:12 NIV).

"At the same time that Christ Jesus warns us of the tribulations we will come across, he also comforts us and shows us who we are to look to for power to overcome our enemies. 'I have told you these things so that you may have peace. In the world you will have trouble. But take heart! I have overcome the world'" (John 16:33 NIV).

Knowing that Jesus overcame the world does not make our walk with the Lord easy. We come across difficulties and problems, it seems, when we barely get started on the work we are called to do. So many times we try to fight back using our own willpower. We may even succeed, for a short time, in defeating our spiritual enemies. To our dismay, the enemy comes back repeatedly with much more intensity each time. During these struggles, many of us forget where the true power comes from. We set our eyes and mind on our problems and become so absorbed in trying to overcome them. The work we are called to do is then left undone. When our problems continue to buzz with life, our minds become confused and afraid. Finally, when the battle becomes too much for us to handle, we must search for the one whose battle it really is. Jesus is there all the time, but we fail to see him because our eyes are focused on our troubles. When we turn back to him, he instantly appears. At first, we may feel that he is angry with us. To our surprise, he rids us of our problems and accepts us readily.

I would like to point out that during most of the difficulties and problems we come across, our minds are attacked to uproot the word of God in our hearts. The enemy, Satan, is still trying his old tricks of getting us to doubt the Word of God just as he caused Eve to doubt in the garden of Eden. "But I am afraid that just as Eve was deceived by the serpent's cunning, your minds may somehow be led astray from your sincere and pure devotion to Christ" (2 Corinthians 11:3 NIV). We must prepare ourselves ahead of time so that we will know what God really does say and mean. We prepare ourselves by reading, meditating, and applying the Word of God to our lives. By preparing this way, we begin to build a spiritual fence about our life to keep the enemy away.

"Therefore I urge you, brothers, in view of God's mercy, to offer your bodies as living sacrifices, holy and pleasing to God—this is your spiritual act of worship. Do not conform any longer to the pattern of this world, but be transformed by the renewing of your mind. Then you will be able to test and approve what God's will is—his good, pleasing, and perfect will" (Romans 12:1–2 NIV).

In the vision, Jesus had commanded to start digging a fence post hole, but it seemed like he was also saying mailbox post hole. The fence is a type of defense against the enemy; reading and studying the scriptures. The mailbox is communication with God; our prayers and supplications. The enemy, Satan, does not want us to study and meditate on the scriptures or have any contact with our God. He wants to stop us before we can even start the practice of reading, studying, meditating, and praying always. A word of comfort; although we intend to read the scriptures and pray, we often fail. At the first sign of trouble we abandon the Word of God. We decide to get back to the Word of God when our troubles intensify, but we are afraid that he will be angry with us, especially if our troubles have become great enough to cause us to sin. We know that the sting of sin is death. We tend to forget Jesus died for our sins. He was tempted in the same ways as we are, but did not sin. He defeated death and sin when he rose from the dead. Believing and looking to him, our sins are forgiven. He does not become angry with us when we turn to him for deliverance, but becomes angry at the cause of our troubles. He lovingly waits for us to realize that, apart from him, we are powerless. It is when we turn back to him that our troubles seem to dissipate before our eyes.

A Dream of Bearing Much Fruit

I had a dream one night that I was in a kitchen cooking. The food I was cooking looked strange and unfamiliar. I have never seen food that looked like this in my entire life. I then saw myself in the garden picking some of the fruit I was cooking. The fruit grew on a vine and had the yellow color of a banana, only brighter. It appeared to look like a large slender trumpet flower. I could see bees flying into the opening, at the top, as they gathered pollen from the inside bottom of the fruit flower. To cook this strange fruit, long strips were cut lengthwise, dipped into a prepared batter, and then fried in hot oil. The taste of it was sweet like honey. Bending down to pick one of

these pieces of fruit, I heard a voice behind me saying, "Make sure that you pick the fruit before the end
closes. Once the end closes, the bees will be trapped
inside. When they die, the fruit will begin to die and
it will be unfit to eat, as it will become poisonous.
Do not be afraid of the bees because they are needed
to pollinate the fruit. Without them, the flowers will
not pollinate and if not pollinated it will not produce
fruit. Eventually the flowers will wither and die. Just
as bees are needed to pollinate the flowers of an apple
tree to cause the flower to become an apple, so are
bees needed for other fruits as well. What a joyous
thing to pick an apple when it is ripe for food, but
how sad when the apple is not picked when ripe and
used as food. If left on the tree, it will soon fall to the
ground and begin to rot. Care must be taken when
the apple is maturing to guard it from birds and
worms. If we let the birds and worms get to it, the
fruit will be marred and eventually become useless."

Comment

In this dream, I believe as Christians we are being
commanded by the Lord to abide in him so that we
may bring forth much fruit. "This is to my Father's
glory, that you bear much fruit, showing yourselves

to be my disciples" (John 15:8 NIV). "But the fruit of the Spirit is love, joy, peace, patience, kindness, goodness, faithfulness, gentleness, and self-control. Against such things there is no law" (Galatians 5:22–23 NIV).

In the first part of the dream about the yellow fruit, the vine is Jesus. The branches that bear fruit are Christians. The fruit is the fruit of the spirit growing in the lives of believers as they grow in faith. The bees represent trials, troubles, and temptations that occur in our lives. The taste of the fruit is the sweetness we experience in our lives when we share our fruit with others. The oil represents the anointing of the Holy Spirit. The dipping of the fruit in batter represents our total and complete commitment to Jesus as the Lord of our lives or baptism. The cutting of the fruit means spiritual circumcision. "I am the vine; you are the branches. If a man remains in me and I in him, he will bear much fruit; apart from me you can do nothing" (John 15:5 NIV). "No discipline seems pleasant at the time, but painful. Later on, however, it produces a harvest of righteousness and peace for those who have been trained by it" (Hebrews 12:11 NIV).

"In him you were also circumcised, in the putting off of the sinful nature, not done by the hands of men but by Christ, having been buried with him in baptism and raised with him through your faith in the power of God, who raised him from the dead" (Colossians 2:11–12 NIV).

When we accept the Lord into our hearts, we become as a branch on the true vine. Our fruit does not come about all at once, but starts as a flowering bud. The Word of God, planted in our hearts, begins to bloom. It is during this time in our walk with the Lord that everything seems so sweet and beautiful. It is like we are looking at a flowering tree in the springtime after experiencing the cold and deadness of winter. Suddenly, trials and troubles come our way. We may sometimes think as Christians we should never have to experience anything bad. Many of us want to stay as a flower the rest of our lives. If nothing bad ever happened to us, we would never learn from our experiences and our flower would wither and die, never to become fruit for others to enjoy. The Scriptures say that Jesus learned obedience by the things he suffered. When troubles come into our life, we learn many things from the Lord and the flower in our heart is pollinated. This is the beginning, of the process, of growing in the Lord. Fruit is never mature at its birth, but must continue to grow until it reaches full maturity. When the fruit of the spirit reaches maturity in our life, we must use it as fruit for others. It is beneficial for us to use our fruit to enrich the lives of others—thus producing more fruit for ourselves. Fruit has many seeds which, if planted in the rich soil of the hearts of others, grows much more fruit. If we let the fruit in our lives reach maturity but do not use it to feed others, our fruit will become overripe and begin to rot. We may even lose our fruit like when an apple falls from a tree and rots on the ground. If we do not pick the apple up immediately after it falls on the ground, it will begin to rot and is no longer eatable. If left rotting on the ground long enough, it will eventually be unrecognizable as fruit. Many of us reach a point in our Christian lives when we need to reach out and feed others with our fruit. We fail to use our fruit for others because we have been troubled by trials, tribulations, and temptations, which make us bitter. All those troubles are good for us so that we might bear fruit. If we do not use the fruit the Lord grows in our lives to feed others, bitterness, hatred, jealousies, etc., become trapped within our hearts just as the bees were trapped in the heart of the fruit flower. Eventually, the fruit produced in our hearts begins to rot and die, becoming useless; it may even become poisonous.

The second part of the dream reinforces the need to learn and grow from the bad things that happen to us. God allows certain circumstances to arise in our life in order for us to mature and bear fruit. He warns us to pray always, to worship, fellowship etc., to guard our fruit. If we do not guard our fruit, the troubles we come across in our Christian walk will eat away at us like worms and birds eat away apples and other fruit. These troubles will not consume us if left unguarded, but will mar us on the inside in our hearts—like worms in an apple. On the outside, our relationships become like birds pecking holes to reach the fruit inside an apple. When we allow ourselves to become marred, we are not whole anymore.

"Consider it pure joy, my brothers, whenever you face trials of many kinds, because you know that the testing of your faith develops perseverance. Perseverance must finish its work so that you may be mature and complete, not lacking anything" (James 1:2–4 NIV).

"See to it that no one misses the grace of God and that no bitter root grows up to cause trouble and defile many" (Hebrews 12:15 NIV). God has given each of us special gifts and abilities. He becomes saddened when we let circumstances in our life eat away at us and we do not use the fruits of the Spirit we have gained to feed other hearts and souls. How joyful he becomes then when we use those fruits for the benefit of others.

"Do not let any unwholesome talk come out of your mouths, but only what is helpful for building others up according to their needs, that it may benefit those who listen. And do not grieve the Holy Spirit of God, with whom you were sealed for the day of redemption. Get rid of all bitterness, rage and anger, brawling and slander, along with every form of malice. Be kind and compassionate to one another, forgiving each other, just as in Christ God forgave you" (Ephesians 4:29–32 NIV).

A Dream of the Gift
of the Holy Spirit

I received a strange dream one night. In the dream, my husband and I had just finished moving into an apartment. It seemed like an apartment, in the sense, that most of the time apartments do not represent a permanent dwelling place. A bought home would be a more permanent dwelling place. When we had finished moving everything into our apartment, I decided to go outside for a while and rest. I was tired and weary. I thought the fresh air would help to revive me. Evening was fast approaching as I stood on the lawn next to a swing set and the sky was becoming increasingly darker. Looking up into the sky, I saw what seemed to be some kind of rocket or missile. It resembled fire; it was yellowish-white and red in color. The colors of the fire were like the fire of a rocket during liftoff. I remember thinking to myself as I watched this fire in the sky, *Oh no! The United States just shot off a missile!* Continuing to watch, I noticed the fire wasn't leaving the earth but was headed for the earth, and I thought maybe a missile was being shot at the United States. I kept staring at it when I was alarmed to realize it was headed straight toward me. I was extremely frightened and grabbed onto the swing set, clinging to it, and trying to bury my head in my arms. Standing there terrified, I dared to look up. I was eager to see how close this rocket was to my presence. To my surprise, it was not like fire now but looked like a gigantic spherical cloud. The cloud, as it approached, made me extremely afraid. It was almost on top of me and I could not move because of my fright. The cloud then landed and totally engulfed my whole being. Immediately I felt peaceful and rested in this strange presence. The peace I felt cannot be described in human words. The whole experience was so overwhelming and calming. I wanted to stay inside this cloud forever. Resting peacefully, I heard a voice coming from within the cloud. The voice seemed as if there were three people talking, but their voices were so blended and unified they became as one voice. The voice, the authority of which was undeniable, began to speak to me saying, "You must warn the people. You must warn the people. For judgment is coming upon the world. There will be many earthquakes and famines in places that have never known such things with increasing intensity. There will be earthquakes in places that have never had earthquakes before. There will be famines in places that have never had famines before. There will be storms and disasters with increasing frequency. There will be fires in places that have not had fires before. There will be many and varied wars in diverse places. Many new diseases will arise that will have *no* cure. You must warn the people *especially* those who think they are going to Heaven, but are *not*." The voice described many other calamities that would come, but I could not remember what they were once I awoke from this dream. I could not remember all the diseases he spoke of after I awoke. The voice then repeated the opening statement, "You must warn the people."

The cloud then began to rise and I felt sad because I did not want this presence to depart from me. I had never known such perfect peace. While watching the cloud leave, I began to talk to myself saying, "No one is going to believe me. They will all think I am crazy. How will anyone believe something as unbelievable as this? I *need* some kind of evidence." I decided to go inside and tell my husband what had just happened; all the while I was thinking how crazy this would seem to him. He would not believe me. I needed some kind of evidence. I told my husband, anyway, despite my doubts. I had to share this incredible experience. I was not surprised when he started laughing at me as if I had lost my mind. I then became severely depressed. I was so depressed that I slumped to the floor and lay there for some time. All hope and joy seemed lost forever. Lying on the floor, I found myself looking out the window. I was hoping to see the cloud I had been in earlier. Suddenly, the same fire I had seen previously appeared in the sky. This time I was not afraid, but I eagerly rushed outside.

The cloud descended upon me again as it had the first time. I heard the voice say to me, "We heard you. We know you need evidence and are taking you to get that evidence. The evidence you will receive is not of the world, but is in the world." The cloud then began to lift me up. Higher and higher, I rose with it into the heavens and beyond. I soon realized that I was in an unfamiliar place. I had never, in my entire life, seen anything like this place. Everything was pure and white. It seemed like a building, but I could not see any walls. There were beings there clothed in white robes and resembling humans. One of the men came up to me and told me to follow him. I can't remember if his mouth moved when he spoke, or if I was able to comprehend in my mind what he was speaking. I observed that the floor was white as I followed this man. The floor was the purest white I had ever seen. It was almost transparent and seemed to radiate its own light. The man I was following took me to one end of the building. There was a stand of some kind located in front of us. The stand was square on top and stood about three feet in height. The man I had followed called another man to bring something to him. The second man brought a rock over and placed it on the stand, and then the first man picked the rock up and told me to take it. It looked like an ordinary rock—the type one might find in the mountains. The man then said, "This is not an ordinary rock, although it might appear that way to you. It is found in the earth but it is not of the earth. There is an ingredient in it that is not found in any other rock upon the earth. This rock can become food when hot water is poured upon it." The man then demonstrated what he meant by taking a small piece of the rock in a clean white bowl that another man had brought to him as he was speaking to me. He called for a pitcher of hot water and told me to watch. The rock began to change as he poured the steaming water on it. Soon it was not a rock any longer, but became some sort of food. The appearance of the food looked like small round cereal flakes soaked in milk—somewhat like a porridge or oatmeal. The man who had given me the rock said, "You must take this to the scientists of the earth and tell them that it has an ingredient in it that is not found anywhere else on earth because it does not come from earth."

I did as he instructed because I found myself in a room full of scientists. I told the scientists that the rock had an ingredient in it that is not found anywhere on earth. I told them that with this ingredient, the rock can change into food when hot water is poured over it. The scientists took the rock and began to examine it. While trying to analyze the rock, they would break off a piece and study it by various means using microscopes and different chemicals. They discovered it did have an ingredient in it which they could not identify. This led them to conclude it was not from the earth. They became obsessed with studying the rock because they desperately wanted to identify this ingredient. I kept yelling at them not to worry about what the ingredient was, but to just pour hot water on it. Someone did pour hot water on it and became more intent on studying it when he saw it turn to food. The scientists became so caught up with studying the rock they could not hear me telling them to pour hot water on it and just use it for food. I stood watching the scientists break the rock, smashing it into little pieces, and hand a small piece to each scientist to study. They did this repeatedly, dissecting the rock by various means and studying it. I grew weary of watching them and walked out, saying to myself, "Oh well, although they have broken this rock up into pieces, I have a whole locker full of the same kind of rock to take to others." I felt sorry for the scientists because they did not listen. "Maybe it is time to move on and take this rock to others. It is to be hoped that some will listen."

Comment

This dream represents the gift of the Holy Spirit. This is what the apostles were told by Jesus to wait for in Jerusalem. He told them to wait for the promise of his father. He had appeared to many of his disciples during the forty days—from the time he was risen, until the day of Pentecost. On one of those occasions, he had told the apostles that John the Baptist had baptized with water, but that they would be baptized with the Holy Spirit as found in the first chapter of Acts (NIV). The apostles, after receiving the gift of the Holy Spirit, then proclaimed to others how they could receive this gift.

"Peter replied, 'Repent and be baptized, every one of you, in the name of Jesus Christ for the forgiveness of your sins, And you will receive the gift of the Holy Spirit. The promise is for you and your children, and for all who are far off—for all whom the Lord our God will call' (Acts 2:38–39 NIV).

"When the apostles in Jerusalem heard that Samaria had accepted the word of God, they sent Peter and John to them. When they arrived, they prayed for them that they might receive the Holy Spirit because the Holy Spirit had not yet come upon any of them. They had simply been baptized into the name of the Lord Jesus. Then Peter and John placed their hands on them and they received the Holy Spirit" (Acts 8:14–17 NIV).

While Apollos was at Corinth, Paul took the road through the interior and arrived at Ephesus. There he found some disciples and asked them, "Did you receive the Holy Spirit when you believed?" They answered, "No, we have not heard that there is a Holy Spirit." So Paul asked, "Then what baptism did you receive?"

"John's baptism," they replied.

"Paul said, 'John's baptism was a baptism of repentance.' He told the people to believe in the one coming after him, that is, in Jesus. On hearing this, they were baptized into the name of the Lord Jesus. When Paul placed his hands on them, the Holy Spirit came on them and they spoke in tongues and prophesied" (Acts 19:1–6 NIV).

Many of us accept the Word of God and are baptized in the name of the Jesus, but we have not asked for and received the Holy Spirit. We may see things happening to our fellow Christians when they receive this gift and become frightened because we do not understand. We may even find ourselves hiding from the spirit of God because of this fear and misunderstanding.

In the dream, the apartment represents our searching in life for something permanent. Our permanent dwelling place will be heaven. The night represents a dark time in life. Looking up into the sky symbolizes the search for more of the Lord in our lives. Seeing the fire in the sky and having fearful thoughts about what it is shows how many of us want, but fear the Holy Spirit. Clinging to the swing set represents clinging to our childish thoughts concerning the Holy Spirit. Our first thought at seeing the Holy Spirit at work in others is usually negative or questionable. We don't see him as he really is. Just like in the dream, the fire was perceived as something that brings destruction. There are many people who still think that the gift of tongues is from the devil. As in the dream, when the spirit of God approaches us, we become frightened, and turn away because we want to hang on to our childish ways. Many of us may become curious enough to dare to look up again. To our surprise, the gift of the Holy Spirit is something totally different from what we first thought. When the Holy Spirit falls on us, he surrounds and fills us with his presence. At that moment we realize how much rest and peace we were missing in our lives without him. The Holy Spirit also gives us gifts and abilities to lift up, edify, and feed his church as in the twelfth chapter of 1 Corinthians (NIV). In the dream, the three voices as one represent God's trinity: Father, Son, and Holy Spirit. The spirit of God, which seemed like fire and yet also like a cloud, reminds me of Exodus 13:21 (NIV), which says, "By day the Lord went ahead of them in a pillar of cloud to give them light, so that they could travel day or night." When the cloud departed from the dream, it does not mean that the spirit of God departs from us. The complete engulfing represents the fullness of God's spirit; an anointing for a commission by God. We receive power from on high so we can carry out our commission. We can be assured that God leaves himself with us when we are baptized because he hears our thoughts and promised he would never leave us. The apostle Paul stated in Hebrews 13:5 (NIV), "Never will I leave you, never will I forsake you."

"For who among men knows the thoughts of a man except the man's spirit within him? In the same way, no one knows the thoughts of God except the Spirit who is from God, that we may understand what God has freely given us" (1 Corinthians 2:11–12 NIV).

"And I will ask the father and he will give you another counselor to be with you forever—the Spirit of truth. The world cannot accept him because it neither sees him nor knows him, but you know him, for he lives with you and will be in you" (John 14:16–17 NIV).

The rock in the dream represents the word of God, that is, the Holy Bible. It is Jesus the word made flesh. "In the beginning was the Word, and the Word was with God, and the Word was God" (John

1:1 NIV). "The Word became flesh and made his dwelling among us" (John 1:14 NIV). The hot water represents the Holy Spirit.

"When the kindness and love of God our Savior appeared, he saved us, not because of righteous things we had done, but because of his mercy. He saved us through the washing of rebirth and renewal by the Holy Spirit, whom he poured out on us generously through Jesus Christ our Savior, so that, having been justified by his grace, we might become heirs having the hope of eternal life" (Titus 3:4–7 NIV).

The pouring of the hot water on the rock and the rock turning into food is the anointing of the Holy Spirit upon the Word of God, which produces food for the soul. This food is the heavenly manna.

"Our forefathers ate manna in the desert; as it is written, 'He gave them bread from heaven to eat.' Jesus said to them, 'I tell you the truth, it is not Moses who has given you the bread from heaven, but it is my Father who gives you the true bread from heaven. For the bread of God is he who comes down from heaven and gives life to the world'" (John 6:31–33 NIV).

Without the gift of the Holy Spirit, our lives become unsettled and somewhat darkened. During these dark times, many of us start searching for a deeper relationship with the Lord. Although we are afraid, we are also curious about the gift of the Holy Spirit. When we do receive the gift of the Holy Spirit, our hearts become restful and full of peace. Many times, as young Christians, we become depressed shortly after this first meeting with the spirit of God. This depression comes about as we try to tell our loved ones about our experience with Jesus and the gift of the Holy Spirit. We know that we need evidence because no one believes us. The evidence comes to us as we read the Word of God, receive it into our hearts, and ask the Holy Spirit to anoint that word, so that it will become food for our souls. Beginning to partake of this food causes our spiritual bodies to be nourished. When the unbelievers of the world watch, they notice there is something different about us. They have to wonder how, all of a sudden, we have words of knowledge and wisdom. We begin to show the gifts and fruits of the spirit to the world and they can't understand it. They try to smash and dissect the Word of God. They try to explain, in scientific terms, what the Word of God contains that other books do not contain. Usually, when we reach this point in our Christian life, we do not become as easily depressed. If those whom we show the Word of God do not want to listen, we press on and take it to those who will. The Word of God, stored in our hearts, is like the locker full of rocks in the dream. It is available to us at any time so that we may share it with others. "I have given them your word and the world has hated them, for they are not of the world any more than I am of the world" (John 17:14 NIV). The part of the dream when the Lord tells me to warn the people reminds me of the twenty-fourth chapter of Matthew (NIV). I suggest that you read the whole chapter.

A Dream about the Church

I received a dream in the night. In this dream, I found myself in the desert. I looked and saw a building in the midst of this desert. The building resembled a church but the construction was not complete. There was still a little more work to be done on the church before it would be finished.

The steeple and a few other areas of the church were still under construction as I could see areas that were not quite complete. I saw many workers building this church. They would fetch stones and add them to the unfinished portions of the building trying desperately to finish on time. The shape of the church was perfect, but the appearance of it was not very beautiful. The shape reminded me of the type of cathedrals one might see on a Christmas card or in a historic sites brochure—possibly like the Sistine Chapel. The color of it appeared like dark sand and it was extremely dull. There was nothing shiny or beautiful to be noticed on any part of the building. I perceived that the work on the building was progressing slowly, too slowly. Many of the workers were extremely weary because of a lack of water in this barren place. There were no trees to provide shade from the hot sun and the workers began to slow down even more. Some of the workers were fainting from lack of water and some just quit building. I felt sorry for the workers; many died. They were trying so hard but to no avail. Suddenly, I heard a voice say, "Stretch forth thy hand." I looked up and could see the arm of a man with the hand stretched forth. Instantly, the desert began to change. Trees and plants were starting to appear everywhere I looked. In the midst of the trees and plants, springs of water were bubbling forth becoming great pools. Each pool of water created appeared to look like an oasis in the desert. Streams and rivers were flowing in several places. There was still much desert, but it was filled more than a third of the way with pools of water, streams, trees, and plants. I turned my head again and saw the same hand stretch forth toward the church. In an instant the church, instead of looking drab and dull, became glorious. The color of the stones were many and varied. Each one glistened like precious jewels—like diamonds, rubies, and gemstones shining in the sun. Its brilliance was almost blinding. The church was alive with a special beauty that cannot be described in words.

Comment

I believe this dream represents where the church of God has been spiritually in these last years. When I say Church of God, I'm referring to believers everywhere no matter what denomination. These believers, in Jesus, make up the true church of God. We have all been in a dry and thirsty land spiritually. This dryness has caused the workers, who continue to build upon the church, to become weary and their work has slowed. Many faint for lack of spiritual water, and many just give up and quit. Some have died and await the resurrection. God will not allow this to continue because of his compassion for his church. Soon he is going to stretch forth his hand and cause streams to appear in the desert of our lives. Christians will be refreshed by these spiritual streams. The streams represent rivers of living waters. The outstretched hand represents the arm of God coming to save us by pouring out his spirit upon us. The church will soon be completed as the last souls are brought in. Once the church is almost complete, God will stretch forth his hand toward his church, pouring out his spirit abundantly to prepare it as the bride of Christ. Each person within the church will then become as a precious stone to God, shiny and bright. Here are a few scriptures that refer to this time:

"Say to those with fearful hearts, "Be strong, do not fear; your God will come, he will come with vengeance; with divine retribution he will come to save you." Then will the eyes of the blind be opened and ears of the dead be unstopped. Then will the lame leap like a deer and the mute tongue shout for joy. Water will gush forth in the wilderness and streams in the desert. The burning sand will become a pool, the thirsty ground bubbling springs. In the haunts where jackals once lay, grass and reeds and papyrus will grow" (Isaiah 35:4–7 NIV).

"For I will pour water on the thirsty land, and streams on the dry ground; I will pour out my Spirit on your offspring and my blessing on your descendants" (Isaiah 44:3 NIV).

"As you come to him, the living Stone—rejected by men but chosen by God and precious to him—you also, like living stones, are being built into a spiritual house to be a holy priesthood, offering spiritual sacrifices acceptable to God through Jesus Christ (1 Peter 2:4–5 NIV).

Visions for the Church

I had three visions during worship in church one night. It was the Thursday before Good Friday, 1987. We partook of communion that night and worshipped the Lord all evening. During the first vision, I had my eyes open when something caught my attention. I could see something moving out of the corner of my eye. I turned and saw a big beautiful butterfly. It was silver with a shimmery appearance—somewhat like seeing sunlight on waves of water. I watched for a little while as the butterfly flew around the sanctuary. I sensed the Lord saying, "Something new and wonderful is being brought forth, the birth of new things that no one has ever seen or felt before. The birth of new ideas is about to take place in my church."

I then closed my eyes. There was total darkness all around. Fear and dread engulfed me. I saw
thick dark thunderclouds forming. Upon seeing this,
I became extremely saddened by the thought that
there didn't seem to be any light, at all, in the world.
Looking again at the clouds, I could see them moving so that a small round opening appeared in the
center. Out of this hole a beam of light was descending. The beam of light was small in diameter, but was
very bright with a white-yellowish color. I knew this
was a pure light. The beam of light descended upon
me. Slowly, the opening in the clouds grew larger and
larger. The light spread rapidly until the whole sanctuary was lit with this intense light. It kept spreading
farther and farther out until I could not see any darkness except on the fringes of the light far, far away.
Then I looked up and saw the center of the beam of
light. Instead of light, it now appeared as water and
yet it was also pure light. The water began a steady
stream downward upon us, slowly and lightly at first.
It was like a fine mist rain. The light that is water then
began falling down faster and harder with larger and
heavier drops. Soon the clouds could not contain the
moisture within them and a downpour came from
the opening of the clouds—like a stream of water
coming from a faucet at full blast. A more descriptive

picture may be the water from a fire hose turned on at full blast. The pressure of the water was so great it began to form a hole in the ground. It would be like turning a garden hose on at full blast and holding it near the ground until a hole forms in the dirt. The water goes down so far and then bubbles back up, forming a type of fountain you might see on a whale as he spouts water. This is what the stream of water was doing. The diameter of the opening in the clouds grew larger and larger so the water coming down covered increasingly more area. The water that was pouring down was as pure light, but as I watched, the water that bubbled up from the ground was dirty and black. The force of the water became so great that the water bubbling back up kept rising higher and higher until it reached the opening in the clouds. Its appearance became darker and blacker as it rose. Once it reached the opening in the clouds, I saw the pure light descending again in a forceful stream. The light that is water descended where the dirty water had come up from the ground. Then I noticed that the water flowing down took on the appearance of blood. It then bubbled back up to the opening in the clouds. Again, I saw the water that was like pure light flowing down, but this time the water, bubbling back up, was clean and pure. It bubbled up about halfway and came down in a fine mist—like holding a garden hose straight up in the air. The water streams up forcefully then arches and descends softly, forming a sort of water umbrella. This umbrella of rain grew wider and wider. It covered an increasingly larger area just as the light had done previously. The umbrella of water was huge, but there was still darkness on the fringes far, far, away. There was no way I would even think about leaving the protection of this light that was water. There was a feeling of overwhelming peace and joy wherever the light that is rain fell. I could sense the fear and dread of the darkness around the outside edges of the light.

Soon the picture changed again and I could see a brilliant light way off in the distance—like a shiny star in the sky. I could not take my eyes off of it as I watched the light begin to approach me. The light then took on the appearance of a man. I knew this man was Jesus as he was walking toward me. Stopping about five feet away, he held out his hand and said, "Don't be afraid. Come walk with me." I was scared, but had a desire to go with him. He then extended both hands in a loving way, but I was still afraid. I felt so unworthy, so I lowered my head in shame. He moved closer, until he was standing right in front of me and said, "Don't be afraid. Come walk with me." I hesitantly held out my hand and he took it. We turned to walk in the direction he had come. I could see myself walking away with him hand in hand when suddenly, I appeared as a very young girl about the age of five. Continuing to walk with him, I saw this young girl gradually mature into adulthood. She was given the beautiful white wedding gown of a young bride and walked away with her Lord.

Comment

Although I saw myself in these visions, I knew that I represented not only myself but also the whole church of God. Seeing myself in the visions made them more personal for me. God is going to do new and wonderful things for his church. There will be a birth of new ideas. He is going to pierce through the darkness in our souls and rain down righteousness upon us. Jesus is the light that appears in our midst. Through the washing of water, by his word, he will penetrate our very roots, cleansing us from all unrighteousness. The filth in our lives will be brought out and ascend to heaven as soon as we realize that Jesus purifies and makes us clean. Our righteousness, which is from Christ, will rain down on others who are nearby. This will be a time of preparation, washing, and cleansing. Then we will be fit to walk with our Lord into the heavens. Even after all this, we will still be as a small child but as we walk with him, we will mature and become his bride. Here are some scriptures that reveal what God is doing with his church:

"See, the former things have taken place, and new things I declare; before they spring into being I announce them to you" (Isaiah 42:9 NIV).

"Let us draw near to God with a sincere heart in full assurance of faith, having our hearts sprinkled to cleanse us from a guilty conscience and having our bodies washed with pure water" (Hebrews 10:22 NIV).

"You heavens above, rain down righteousness; let the clouds shower it down. Let the earth open wide, let salvation spring up, let righteousness grow with it; I the Lord have created it" (Isaiah 45:8 NIV).

"Husbands, love your wives, just as Christ loved the church and gave himself up for her to make her holy, cleansing her by the washing with water through the word, and to present her to himself as a radiant church, without stain or wrinkle or any other blemish, but holy and blameless" (Ephesians 5:28–27 NIV).

"Let us rejoice and be glad and give him glory! For the wedding of the Lamb has come, and his bride has made herself ready. Fine linen, bright and clean, was given her to wear. (Fine linen stands for the righteous acts of the saints" (Revelation 19:7–8 NIV).

Conclusion

I would like to conclude this book by first adding some words of caution. We must be careful not to let ourselves be led astray by dreams and visions. We must test the spirits, whether they are God.

"This is how you can recognize the Spirit of God; every spirit that acknowledges that Jesus Christ has come in the flesh is from God, but every spirit that does not acknowledge Jesus is not from God… This is the spirit of the antichrist, which you have heard is coming and even now is already in the world" (1 John 4:2–3 NIV).

Not every dream or vision we have is from God. Those that are will be in harmony with the word of God. They will come true, or as the scriptures state, if a dream or vision is from God it will come to pass.

If after careful study we come to the conclusion a particular dream or vision is from God, we must not put our trust in that dream or vision. Our trust must be in Jesus who is the author and finisher of our faith. I stated in chapter four that we have all been given special gifts and abilities which we need to use. We should not become like the wicked servant spoken of by Jesus in Luke 19:12–27 (NIV) who was afraid to use his talent from God to gain more. At the same time, we need to pray for wisdom, knowledge, and guidance to reap the full benefit of those gifts and abilities.

I pray that these dreams and visions you have read will become food for your soul just as they are food for my soul. I hope the gifts the Lord has bestowed upon you will be used to feed others. "Do not neglect your gift, which was given you through a prophetic message when the body of elders laid their hands on you" (1 Timothy 4:14 NIV). Do not be afraid to stir up the gift of God. "For God did not give us the spirit of timidity, but a spirit of power, of love, and of self-discipline" (2 Timothy 1:7 NIV).

Remember, "Every good gift and perfect gift is from above, coming down from the Father of the heavenly Lights, who does not change like shifting shadows" (James 1:17 NIV).

About the Author

Jennifer Truesdale (Jenny) is a full-time employee for a major airline in Tulsa, Oklahoma. She grew up in Englewood, Colorado, where she married her high school sweetheart. She has a grown daughter and son. Her daughter has two boys currently serving in the United States Air Force. Her son is an ordained minister with the Assemblies of God and has three beautiful girls. She continues to talk with anyone who will listen, about dreams and visions God has given her, for the enrichment of the hearer.

9 7 9 8 8 8 6 1 6 1 6 4 9